MAKING CANDLES

Easy to follow Beginner's and advanced procedures for manufacturing your own candles at home

Clement Ahnert

Table of Contents

CHAPTER ONE 3
  An Overview of Making Candles 3

CHAPTER TWO 8
  Gathering Your Supplies 8
  Wicks: Your Candle's Heart 13

CHAPTER THREE 19
  Beyond Containers: Selecting Your Canvas 19
  Tools of the Trade: Equipping Yourself for Success 25

CHAPTER FOUR 30
  Crafting Your Candle Masterpiece 30
  Curing Your Candle: The Art of Waiting 36

CHAPTER FIVE 42
  Beyond the Basics: Advanced Techniques 42
  Scenting Your Way: Perfecting Fragrance in Candles 48

CHAPTER SIX 54

Safety First: Making Confident Candles...54
THE END 59

**Please consider leaving us a review.
Thank you**

CHAPTER ONE
An Overview of Making Candles

Greetings and Welcome to the Candlemaking World

Greetings from the wonderful world of candlemaking! Making candles is a fun and creative activity that may be enjoyed by anybody looking for a creative outlet, a warm and creative hobby, or a unique present option.

A Brief History of Candles

Candles have been a part of human history for thousands of years. They were first made from beeswax by ancient civilizations including the Egyptians, who did so as early as 3000 BC. Candles have changed over time from being useful light sources to becoming emblems of festivity, ritual, and atmosphere. Every era has added to the intricate tapestry of candle manufacture, from the taper candles of the Middle Ages to the fragrant jar candles of the present.

Why Make Your Own Candles Given Their Allure?

Although buying candles from stores is handy, making your own has a unique quality. This is why homemade candles are so appealing:

Personalization: You can customize every element of homemade candles to suit your tastes. You may design candles that express your own sense of style and individuality, from selecting colors and scents to altering the forms and containers.

High-quality ingredients: You have control over the ingredients used when you make your own candles. In contrast to some commercial candles, you can choose premium wax, essential oils, and wicks to ensure a cleaner, longer-lasting burn.

Cost-Effectiveness: Despite common assumption, making candles at home can be less expensive than purchasing them from the shop, particularly if they are manufactured in large quantities. Luxurious candles can be had for a fraction of the price by reusing containers and buying ingredients in larger quantities.

Benefits for Therapy: Making candles is a soothing and stress-relieving activity that can be therapeutic. Creating candles, blending scents, and melting wax may all be contemplative rituals that encourage creativity and mindfulness.

Giving: Thoughtful candles produced by hand are ideal presents for friends and family. A handmade candle soaked with love and care is a wonderful gift for any event, be it a birthday, holiday, or special occasion. Recipients will be delighted.

Prepare to enter a world of creative pleasure and sensual delight as you begin your candle-making journey. We'll go over the necessary supplies, methods, and equipment in the parts that follow so you may make beautiful candles in the convenience of your own home. Prepare to let your creativity run wild and fill your environment with the cozy warmth of handmade candles!

CHAPTER TWO
Gathering Your Supplies

It's crucial to assemble the necessary materials before entering the fascinating realm of candlemaking. A seamless and pleasurable creating process is ensured by having the right supplies on hand, from wax to wicks and everything in between. Let's look at the essential elements you'll require to get going.

Choosing the Best Wax: Synthetic vs. Natural Choices

Selecting the right kind of wax is one of the most important choices in candlemaking. The two primary categories of waxes are natural and synthetic.

Soy Wax: The Sustainable Option

Because it burns cleanly and is environmentally benign, soy wax has become increasingly popular. Soybean oil is a renewable resource that is used to make candles with low soot and toxic emissions, which makes them healthier for the environment and for you. Additionally, soy wax has a great scent throw, which means it can efficiently transfer fragrance oils, producing delightfully fragrant candles.

Beeswax: A Luxurious Touch

Beeswax is a great option for anyone looking for a little extra luxury. Beeswax candles, made by bees, smell faintly of honey and have a naturally occurring golden color. Allergy sufferers and others who are sensitive to artificial aromas will find beeswax candles excellent since they burn cleanly and release negative ions that aid in air purification.

Paraffin Wax: A Timeless Option

Due to its cost and adaptability, paraffin wax has long been used extensively in the candle-making industry. Paraffin wax, which comes from petroleum, is renowned for its strong color retention and superior smell throw. Even though paraffin candles produce more soot than their natural equivalents, technological advancements in the candle industry have produced cleaner-burning formulas with less of an adverse effect on the environment.

Examining Additional Wax Choices: Gel Wax, Coconut Wax, and Additional

Apart from paraffin, beeswax, and soy, there are a few other types of wax to take into account. For example, gel wax provides a translucent, jelly-like look that enables imaginative embeds and designs. Candles made with coconut wax, which is made from coconut oil, have a smooth, creamy texture with a strong aroma throw. By experimenting with various wax mixtures and additives, you can achieve distinctive outcomes and perfectly tailor your candles.

Choose the wax that best fits your interests and ideals by taking into account characteristics like scent throw, burn time, and eco-friendliness when making candles. Now that you have the ideal wax, you can make beautiful candles that will entice the senses and brighten your environment.

Wicks: Your Candle's Heart

Wicks are essential to the process of creating candles because they act as a channel for the evaporated wax that generates the flame. For the best burn performance and a secure and pleasurable candle experience, choosing the correct wick is crucial. Let's explore the world of wicks and determine which one is best for your candle.

Selecting the Appropriate Wick for Your Candle: Sizing Up Your Wick

There is no one-size-fits-all wick; instead, it is determined by a number of variables, such as the type of wax being used, the container's diameter, and the desired burn characteristics. A basic

guide regarding wick sizing is provided below:

Diameter of the Container: Selecting the right wick size for your candle vessel depends heavily on its diameter. Generally speaking, thinner wicks are needed in smaller containers to avoid overheating and sooting, whereas thicker wicks are needed in bigger diameter containers to guarantee adequate wax consumption and an even burn pool.

Type of Wax: Different types of wax have distinct burn qualities that affect the choice of wick. For instance, because of its softer viscosity and lower melt point than paraffin wax, soy wax typically requires larger wicks. To get the perfect wick size for your particular wax formulation, make sure to refer to the wick sizing guidelines supplied by the makers or perform test burns.

Desired Burn Rate: For larger rooms or outdoor use, decide if you want a more strong flame or a gradual, continuous burn. Whereas smaller wicks result in slower, more controlled burns, thicker wicks usually produce greater flames and higher burn rates.

You can choose a wick that encourages the best burn performance and improves the general quality of your candles by carefully evaluating these variables.

Examining Wood, Hemp, and Eco-Friendly Wick Types

Candle producers can experiment with a range of substitute possibilities in addition to conventional cotton wicks:

Eco Wicks: Usually constructed with a paper or cotton core, eco wicks are manufactured from natural cotton fibers. For candle manufacturers who care about the environment, they are a cleaner and more sustainable option because of their design, which reduces carbon buildup and sooting.

Hemp Wicks: Made from organic hemp fibers, hemp wicks have a distinctive visual appeal. They create a consistent flame that improves the atmosphere of your candles by burning slowly and evenly.

Wooden Wicks: Wooden wicks give your candles a more sensory element by producing a crackling sound that is evocative of a warm fireplace. They come in a variety of sizes and forms to fit different candle designs, and they are frequently manufactured from wood that is supplied responsibly.

By experimenting with various wick types, you may customize the burning experience to fit your preferences and style while also adding adaptability and character to your candle creations.

When starting your candle-making endeavors, keep in mind that choosing a wick is a combination of art and science. Enjoy the process of creating candles that burn true and bright, infusing your room with warmth and aroma. Take the time to experiment with different wick sizes and kinds to discover the ideal match for your candles.

**Please consider leaving us a review.
Thank you**

CHAPTER THREE
Beyond Containers: Selecting Your Canvas

In candle production, the vessel you choose is more than just a holding for wax—it's a vital aspect of your candle's aesthetic appeal and functionality. The choices are unlimited, ranging from traditional jars to unusual containers. Let's investigate the world of candle holders and learn how to pick the ideal surface for your crafts.

Traditional Candle Jars: Practicality and Style

Candle jars are a timeless choice for candle production, delivering a great balance of efficiency and elegance. Candle jars offer a sleek and elegant appearance that goes well with any type of design. They come in a variety of sizes, styles, and materials, including glass and ceramic. Because of their transparency, the beauty of the wax and flame is also able to be seen, producing an amazing visual display.

When choosing candle jars, take into account elements like:

Size: Select a jar size that will fit nicely in your location and hold the quantity of wax you intend to use.

Material: Ceramic jars offer a hint of elegance, while glass jars are traditional and adaptable. Think about the durability and aesthetics of various materials.

Closure: To maintain the scent and extend the life of your candles, use jars with tight-fitting lids or covers.

Tins, Mugs, and Unusual Containers: Adding Character to Your Candles

Candle containers come in a far wider variety than just jars for individuals who want a more unique and customized look. There are so many different ways to give your candles flair and charm, including mugs, tins, teacups, and even antique vessels. When recycled once the candle burns down, these unusual containers not only make for eye-catching decor items but also offer a joyful surprise to the receivers.

When looking at substitute candle holders, take into account:

Theme: Select vessels that complement the atmosphere or theme you wish to create with your candles. There's a container to fit every style, be it modern, rustic, or vintage.

Practicality: Make sure the containers you've selected can hold hot wax and flames and are resistant to heat. Steer clear of items that could break or crack in a hot environment.

Versatility: Choose receptacles that are simple to use again once the candle has been consumed. Give your containers, whether they are storage jars or plant pots, a purpose other than candlemaking.

Selecting Heat-Resistant Containers for Candle Safety

Safety is the most important consideration while creating candles, regardless of the kind of container you select. To avoid mishaps and to feel at ease, always choose containers that are resistant to heat and can endure the heat produced by burning candles.

Metal, glass, and ceramic containers are common options because of their strength and ability to withstand heat. To be sure that the containers you have selected can securely contain the flame's heat without melting, breaking, or creating other risks, you must, nevertheless, carry out extensive testing.

You and your loved ones can make candles that are not only aesthetically pleasing but also safe and delightful to burn by carefully choosing candle containers that combine aesthetic appeal with usefulness and safety. So, unleash your imagination as you select the ideal canvas for your candle-making endeavors and investigate the plethora of options available for candle containers!

Tools of the Trade: Equipping Yourself for Success

Having the proper instruments will let you start your candle-making journey with confidence and creativity. Possessing the right tools will put you in a successful position, from properly melting wax to guaranteeing accurate measurements and upholding a secure work atmosphere. Let's look at the basic tools of the trade and how you may use them to further your candlemaking efforts.

The Humble Double Boiler: A Safe Way to Melt Wax

A bain-marie, or double boiler, is a vital candlemaking instrument that securely melts wax without the use of direct heat.

The double boiler, which consists of two nested pots or containers with one filled with water and the other with wax, uses indirect, low heat to melt wax evenly without scorching or overheating.

In the event of a double boiler:

Pick the Correct Size: Make sure the double boiler you choose is big enough to hold the quantity of wax you want to melt without spilling or overflowing.

Keep Up Constant Supervision: When the wax is melting, never leave the double boiler unsupervised. To avoid overheating, keep a careful eye on the temperature and adjust the heat as necessary.

Prevent Water from Contacting the Wax: Water, even a tiny bit of it, might cause the wax to seize or become contaminated. Therefore, be sure that no water comes into touch with the wax.

You may create beautifully sculpted candles by melting wax securely and effectively by learning how to use a double boiler.

Safety equipment, mixing utensils, and thermometers

A double boiler is not the only essential tool for successful candlemaking; the following are also essential:

Thermometers: To make sure your wax reaches the right melting and pouring temperatures, you must keep an eye on its temperature with a trustworthy thermometer. Because of their accuracy and user-friendliness, digital or candy thermometers are frequently utilized.

Mixing Tools: To incorporate fragrance oils, colors, and additives into the melted wax, use stirring sticks, spatulas, or specialized tools for creating candles. To prevent contamination, use non-reactive materials like silicone or stainless steel.

Safety Equipment: Use protective equipment, such as heat-resistant gloves, aprons, and safety goggles, to shield oneself from potential dangers. Using these supplies can lessen the risk of burns, spillage, and exposure to dangerous chemicals when manufacturing candles.

You can make candles with accuracy, effectiveness, and peace of mind if you arm yourself with these crucial equipment and safety gear. Always put safety first, and relish the satisfying feeling of realizing your creative thoughts for candles!

CHAPTER FOUR
Crafting Your Candle Masterpiece

From melting wax to pouring your masterpiece, we'll walk you through every step of the candle-making process so you can start with confidence. Get ready to let your imagination run wild and realize your idea under the cozy glow of candles.

Setting the Scene and Organizing Your Workspace

Clean and Organize: Make sure that everything you need is easily accessible, and remove any clutter from your desk. A spotlessly tidy workspace creates the ideal atmosphere for a flawless candle-making process.

Protective Measures: Put on your safety gear, such as goggles and gloves that can withstand heat, to shield yourself from any potential risks while creating candles.

Ventilation: To disperse any fumes released during the melting and pouring of wax, make sure your workspace has enough ventilation.

Melting Wax: A Secure and Managed Procedure

To set up your double boiler, put water in the bottom pot and set it over medium heat on the stove. To ensure even melting, place the wax in the top pot and let it melt slowly, stirring from time to time.

Keep an Eye on the Temperature: Make sure the wax reaches the required melting point for the particular kind of wax you're using by using a thermometer to keep track of its temperature. Steer clear of overheating since this might deteriorate aroma oils and lower the candle's quality.

Adding Fragrance and Color to Make Your Candle Personalized

Color Selection: To get the color you choose, you can add liquid or candle dye chips to the melted wax. To get the appropriate shade, start with a little bit and apply more gradually.

Fragrance Blend: To uniformly disperse the aroma, add fragrance or essential oils to the melted wax and stir. To prevent overwhelming the smell or undermining the candle's integrity, pay attention to the appropriate fragrance load for the wax you have chosen.

Putting the Wick on: Making Sure It Burns Clean

To secure the wick, rapidly center it at the bottom of the candle container after dipping its metal base into the melted wax. Securing the wick in the center of the container, hold it in place until the wax solidifies.

Use Wick Holders: During the pouring process, keep the wick centered and erect by using wick holders or adhesive dots for increased stability.

Pouring the Candle: Accuracy and Waiting Time

Get Ready to Pour: To avoid frosting or sinkholes, take the wax off the heat source as soon as it reaches the appropriate temperature and color. Then, let it cool somewhat.

Pouring Technique: Using caution to ensure a steady stream and prevent spills or splashes, carefully pour the molten wax into the prepared candle container. Allow a tiny space to exist at the top of the container so that expansion and adequate cooling can occur.

Final Touches: After the candle has fully cooled and solidified, trim the wick to the appropriate length. To make your masterpiece candle even more unique, add embellishments, charms, or labels.

You've taken basic components and turned them into a gorgeous, handcrafted candle that is ready to fill your area with warmth and aroma with a little perseverance, accuracy, and artistic flair. Savor the atmosphere created by your candle's flickering light and bask in the satisfaction of making something genuinely one-of-a-kind.

Curing Your Candle: The Art of Waiting

Congratulations on creating such a superb candle! It's time to be patient now and let your creation go through the very important curing procedure. For your candle to set correctly, develop its full aroma throw, and burn as efficiently as possible, it must be cured. Let's examine the significance of curing, comprehend the duration of curing for various wax kinds, and resolve typical curing problems.

Curing Is Important to Let Your Candle Set Correctly

After pouring, the process of curing—also referred to as setting or cooling—is when your candle stabilizes and solidifies. Even while it could be tempting to fire your candle right away, waiting a few days will guarantee that the wax solidifies completely, the aroma oils are thoroughly incorporated, and any possible problems are resolved before burning.

Curing has various advantages, such as:

Better Scent Throw: During the curing process, letting the fragrance oils mix with the wax improves the candle's scent throw, giving it a stronger, longer-lasting perfume when burned.

Decreased Frosting and Sinkholes: By allowing the wax to cool and solidify uniformly, curing helps avoid typical problems like frosting—a whitish, crystalline look on the surface of the candle—and sinkholes, which are sunken spots in the core of the candle.

Improved Burn Performance: Candles that have been properly cured burn cleaner and more evenly, extending their burn time and reducing wax waste.

Recognizing the Curing Times of Various Types of Wax

The kind of wax you use plus outside variables like humidity and temperature might affect how long your candle takes to cure. Generally speaking:

Soy Wax: It usually takes 24 to 48 hours for soy wax candles to completely cure. To produce the best aroma throw, some fragrance oils, however, might benefit from a prolonged curing period of up to two weeks.

Paraffin Wax: Candles made with paraffin wax typically cure in 12 to 24 hours. But you can get better burn performance and scent throw if you let them cure for an extra day.

Beeswax: Because of their heavier consistency and greater melting point, beeswax candles may take longer to cure. For beeswax candles, allow at least 48 to 72 hours for curing.

In order to determine the proper curing time for your candles, it is imperative that you adhere to the guidelines supplied by the manufacturer of the wax and fragrance oils that you have selected.

Solving Typical Curing Problems

Here are some recommendations for troubleshooting if you run into problems with frosting, uneven cooling, or poor scent throw throughout the curing process:

Uneven Cooling: To encourage even cooling and avoid sinkholes, make sure your candles are positioned on a level, level surface away from drafts or direct sunlight.

Frosting: This is a normal feature of soy wax and several other waxes; it has no bearing on how well a candle works. After curing, wrap your candles in wax paper or store them somewhere cool and dark to reduce frosting.

Bad perfume Throw: If your candle doesn't smell very well after curing, you might want to try adding more fragrance to your wax formulation or curing it longer to give the perfume more time to fully develop.

Through comprehension of the significance of curing, adherence to suggested curing durations, and resolution of frequent problems, you can guarantee that your candles are thoroughly cured and prepared to provide a pleasurable sensory encounter upon lighting. If you are patient, you will soon be basking in the warm glow of a wonderfully cured candle, the result of your labors in manufacturing candles.

CHAPTER FIVE
Beyond the Basics: Advanced Techniques

After you've mastered the foundations of candlemaking, it's time to enhance your skills with more complex methods that give your creations depth, dimension, and visual interest. Discover how to create eye-catching designs by utilizing layers and color to show your ideas in the form of candles.

Stunning Design: Enhance Your Candles with Color and Layers

Dyes, Pigments, and Micas: To create unique color combinations and effects, experiment with a range of coloring agents, such as powdered pigments, liquid dyes, and sparkling micas. By using these adaptable additives, you can give your candles vivid colors, delicate tints, or even iridescent finishes to give them more visual appeal.

Color Blocking: To make visually arresting color blocks, divide your candle container into sections and fill each section with varying colored wax. Try with different color combinations that contrast or complement one another to create eye-catching, visual designs.

Marbling: To obtain a marbled look, swirl two or more colors of heated wax together in the pouring container. Take care not to overmix the colors as you gently swirl them with a skewer or toothpick. Every candle will have a different design that resembles agate or swirling marble.

Embeds and Inclusions: You can incorporate items or inclusions into the wax to give your candles more visual appeal. Think about adding glitter, dried flowers, plants, or other ornamental accents to your candles to make eye-catching focal points.

Colors, Pigments, and Micas: An Examination of Coloring Methods

Liquid Dyes: With just a few drops, you may obtain perfect color saturation with liquid candle dyes, which are convenient and easy to use. Create unique hues by combining dyes or diluting them with fragrance oil to achieve a transparent look.

Powdered Pigments: When combined directly with molten wax, powdered pigments offer rich, opaque colors with a strong color payoff. Try combining several colors to create interesting color effects and variations.

Micas: Micas are minerals that have been finely powdered and give your candles a shine and sparkle. In order to achieve shimmering metallic or iridescent finishes that catch the light and give your candles a glamorous look, mix micas with liquid dyes or directly into melted wax.

Making Layered Candles: An Eye-Catching Color Symphony

Gradient Layers: Fill the candle container with layers of wax in varying colors, letting each one cool and solidify before adding the next. To add depth and visual appeal to the candle, experiment with the thickness and positioning of each layer.

Embedded Layers: To produce dynamic visual effects, embed inclusions or objects within the wax layers. To add dimension to the candle and give it a sense of depth, try layering contrasting colors or materials.

Hidden Layers: Before pouring the main layer into your candles, place a thin layer of colored wax at the bottom of the container. This will allow you to create hidden layers within your candles. The concealed layer will gradually become visible while the candle burns, giving a surprising and intriguing feature.

You can push the boundaries of creativity and sophistication in candlemaking by experimenting with sophisticated techniques including layered candles, brilliant designs, and coloring processes. Try a variety of techniques, hues, and textures to let your creativity run wild and produce candles that are both aesthetically pleasing and fragrant.

Scenting Your Way: Perfecting Fragrance in Candles

Infusing your candles with alluring fragrances gives your making endeavors a new level of complexity. Let's investigate the realm of essential oils and fragrance oils, learn about the significance of fragrance load and flash point, and get some advice on how to get a persistent aroma throw in your candles.

Comparing Fragrance Oils and Essential Oils: Know Your Options

Essential oils: Produced by distilling or cold-pressing plants, essential oils have natural perfumes and medicinal properties. They are available in a broad range of fragrances, including citrus, spice, and floral and herbal. Essential oils can give your candles a more rustic feel, but they can also be more expensive than fragrance oils and have a less aroma throw.

Fragrance oils: Made from synthetic or natural aroma compounds, they offer a wide variety of aromas, including ones that aren't found in the natural world. Fragrance oils have a strong aroma throw and durability and are made especially for manufacturing candles. They are available in a wide range of choices, so you can make personalized mixes and distinctive fragrance combinations.

Ensure Safe and Powerful Fragrance with Flash Point and Fragrance Load

The temperature at which a fragrance oil releases vapor that can catch fire when it comes into contact with an open flame is known as its "flash point." To ensure safety during the candle-making process, it is imperative to use fragrance oils that have a flash point higher than the temperature at which you plan to pour your candles.

The quantity of fragrance oil used in relation to the total amount of wax in your candle recipe is known as the fragrance load. To get maximum smell throw without sacrificing burn performance or safety, it is imperative that you adhere to the specified fragrance load parameters supplied by the manufacturer of the wax and fragrance oils of your choice.

How to Get a Long-Lasting Fragrance Throw

Appropriate Mixing: To guarantee even dispersion, carefully mix aroma oils into the molten wax while swirling gently. Refrain from overmixing, since this may cause air bubbles and compromise the efficacy of the scent.

Cure Time: To ensure that the aroma oils thoroughly mix with the wax and create their perfume throw, let your candles cure for the specified amount of time before burning them. A stronger, longer-lasting scent could be obtained with longer curing durations.

Container Selection: To promote the best possible diffusion of aroma, use containers with a wide aperture and smooth interior surfaces. Steer clear of containers with rough surfaces or narrow necks as these could obstruct the discharge of aroma.

Wick Selection: To guarantee an even burn and maximum fragrance release, use the wick size that corresponds to the size of your candle. A candle with a wick that is the right size will enable it reach a full melt pool, which will facilitate the aroma oils' efficient vaporization and dispersion.

Burn Conditions: To keep the fragrance oils from fading too rapidly, burn your candles in an area that is free of drafts.

Before used, trim the wick to the specified length to get the best possible burn and smell throw.

You can make candles that entice the senses and fill your environment with fascinating fragrances by carefully choosing and utilizing fragrance oils or essential oils, comprehending flash points and fragrance loads, and putting guidelines for generating a long-lasting scent throw into practice. Savor the process of scent-making your way to flawless candle-making!

CHAPTER SIX
Safety First: Making Confident Candles

While making candles is a fun activity, safety should always come first. Let's examine important procedures to guarantee a secure and pleasurable candle-making experience, from fire safety necessities to appropriate candle upkeep.

Essentials of Fire Safety: Safe Candle Burning

Never Leave Unattended: When lighting candles, always keep an eye on them and never leave them alone, especially in places where kids or pets are present.

Keep Away from Flammable items: To avoid unintentional fires, place candles on heat-resistant surfaces far from bedding, drapes, and other flammable items.

Prevent Overcrowding: To provide adequate ventilation and prevent overheating, place candles at least three inches apart.

Use Candle Holders: To ensure that there are no spills, always burn candles in strong, heat-resistant holders that can catch all wax drips.

How to Place Candles Correctly and Prevent Drafts

Stay away from drafts: They can make candles burn unevenly, flicker, or smoke. To guarantee a steady burn, keep candles away from open windows, doors, and vents.

Ideal Location: Set candles on flat, stable surfaces far from busy roads and out of children's and animals' reach.

Be Aware of the Surface: To avoid unintentional fires, make sure the area beneath the candle is clutter-free and heat-resistant.

Keeping Your Burn Clean: Shaping Your Wick

Trim Regularly: To avoid excessive smoking, mushrooming, and uneven burning, trim your candle's wick to about ¼ inch before lighting it.

Use Wick Trimmers: To get a clean, exact cut and prevent fraying or splintering, invest in wick trimmers made especially for candles.

Eliminate Debris: To avoid wick trimmings and debris igniting and resulting in uneven burning, remove them from the surface of the candle before lighting.

How to Put Out a Candle Safely and Never Leave It Alone

Use a Snuffer: To stop hot wax from splattering, extinguish candles with a candle snuffer or soft blowing.

Steer clear of blowing out candles since this can send a gust of air that could spill hot wax or cause the wick to move out of center. Instead, gently put out the flame with a lid or snuffer.

Double-Check: After the flame has been extinguished, be sure there are no embers left and the wick is completely extinguished.

You may create a safe and peaceful space where you can enjoy the comforting glow and alluring scent of your handcrafted candles by following these safety precautions and remaining vigilant during the candle-making process. As you set out on your candle-making excursions, let safety be your beacon of hope!

**Please consider leaving us a review.
Thank you**

THE END